W9-BNG-671

*how to help folks
have fun*

how to

HELP FOLKS

HAVE FUN

HELEN AND LARRY EISENBERG

A book by the authors of *The Handbook of Skits and Stunts; The Family Fun Book;* and *Fun with Stunts,
Skits, and Stories.*

GRAMERCY PUBLISHING COMPANY
New York

introduction

One of the joys of life is found in helping others.

This is a book written to help you to help others have fun and to enjoy the experience yourself, for someone has said, "To be interesting, one must be interested." We have tried here to give suggestions which, if you are a brand-new leader, will enable you to plan social activities that will bring genuine enjoyment to the participants.

A little volume like this should only whet your appetite. If you are really interested in what the right kind of recreation can do to people you will use this book as a springboard to the wealth of resources that are available in every public library and every bookshop.

We are indebted to a number of people for ideas used here, but want to make special acknowledgment to Johnny Hassler for a wealth of party ideas shared with us.

HELEN AND LARRY EISENBERG

table of contents

1

leading folks in fun

what makes a leader popular?

Have you ever watched a recreation leader in action and tried to analyze what makes him well liked? You would find it interesting, and helpful too, to observe not one but several game leaders and to note what they have or what they do in common that makes the group have fun. See if you agree with these points that we have discovered about the usual popular leader:

He is well prepared. He doesn't flounder, trying to think how to break the ice or trying to remember the rules of a new game. He knows that it takes not just practice and experience but hard work ahead of time to hold a successful party.

He is group-minded. He regards himself as a part of the group, even though he is the leader, and so he refers to himself and the group as "we"—thus identifying himself with the group. He does not try to "run" the crowd; he is guided by its wishes. He gets his goals from the group, giving guidance in the process, but he himself has certain objectives in mind for the event. His genuinely democratic attitude draws out the confidence and trust of the group members because they know that he respects them as persons.

He likes people. Therefore he is understanding and friendly. He is tactful and kindly in giving directions and in correcting the players—not sharp-tongued or witty at their expense. He knows that a desire for recognition is one of the basic needs of everybody, and so he expresses appreciation of things well done by individual players. He recognizes that people are different, and so he doesn't assume that everybody will want to take part in all the games, but he tries to offer at least a few activities that they all will enjoy. He knows how to help others have fun. He is sensitive to the needs and moods of the group. At the same time he is pleasantly firm and does not allow the distracting activity of a few to disturb the entire group.

He has valuable personal qualifications or characteristics such as *poise*—he is not thrown off balance by little irritations; *humility*—he is confident but not cocky, and he is not afraid to reveal that he doesn't know everything; *creativeness*—he likes to try new ideas, new patterns, and he is constantly learning from the group. He is a *hard worker* and he asks no one to do something that he would not be willing to do himself. He has a strong *sense of responsibility*. (He is not like the counselor who puffed up the hill and asked everyone along the road, "Did you see a group of little boys go by here? I'm their leader.") He is a *fun lover* himself—and that spirit is, of course, contagious. He has *vision*—he wants the persons in his group to learn and grow through the very activities of the group. He has *religious faith*—a code which recognizes the fatherhood of God and the brotherhood of man, and so he carries out that creed in his relations with all members of the group, believing that they can grow and develop through the right kind of fun as well as through other means.

how do you begin if you are a new leader?

First of all, ask yourself these questions: "If I were coming to this party as a guest, not as a leader, would I enjoy this activity? What would be my state of mind? What would I want the leaders to do to make me feel comfortable when I arrived? or after I had been there a while?"

With these thoughts in mind, line up your activities and decide your program in advance. You may want to start out in the simplest way with games that can be played with the group seated. It is harder to direct a group "on their feets than on their seats."

If the group is large, it is well to break it up into small

units or circles for at least part of the time, so that the experience can be kept personal. That is why square dances and relay races are such fun. Encourage all members of the group to join in the fun, but don't force them to participate actively all the time. Remember that sometimes, especially for elders, it is possible to take part and have fun just by watching a game.

You may have been asked to lead a group over a long period of time—for example, as a club adviser. In that case, an interest finder is useful to discover what recreational activities really interest the members. Get a small committee from the club members to help draw up the questions or items to be checked and, later, to record the answers.

No matter whether you are somebody who has been asked to take charge of the games just one night at a church family party or at the grange meeting, or a scout counselor off on a hike with your group, or a chaperone at a PTA dance, you will benefit from an occasional recreation leadership training course. Ask more experienced leaders in your school, church, club, or agency whether such courses are available in your own or a nearby community.[1] Sometimes in small towns there are monthly voluntary meetings held for swapping ideas. You can start a small library of your own, too, on games, skits, and stunts as a dependable and readily available resource.

You may be wondering, "How can I keep track of all the games and stunts I may want to use sometime?" Here are a few suggestions for organizing your material so that you can find it easily when you need it:

1. *Card file.* This is one of the best ways, whether 3x5, 4x6, or 5x8 cards are used. Each card holds directions for one activity and it is filed in an easy-to-remember category—such as Group Starters, Mixers, Active Games, Less Active Games,

---

[1] Recreation courses are sometimes listed in publications such as *Leisure* (25 cents a year, Box 871, Nashville, Tenn.) and *Recreation Magazine* ($4.00 a year, 315 Fourth Ave., New York, N.Y.).

Songs, Stunts, Equipment Games, Folk Games and Square Dances, Quiz Questions, Contests, Water Games.

2. *File folders or manila envelopes.* Drop into them all recreational ideas, clippings, price lists, drawings, bibliographies, other helps.

3. *Notebook.* Many game leaders carry a small notebook in which game or stunt activities and directions are entered alphabetically under categories.

4. *Marking books.* As you read a book such as this one (if it belongs to you!), mark the more useful ideas, perhaps using a code of your own.

5. *Sample parties.* Some leaders like to block out sample parties in advance, to be used on short notice. (See the two at the end of this chapter.)

6. *Hand cards.* For calling or giving directions, a small hand card for reference, which can be held by the leader almost out of sight, is helpful to some game leaders.

7. *Master songbook.* So many songs come from so many sources that it is well to have at least two "master songbook" collections pasted up if possible—one for you as leader and one for the pianist.

8. *Leader's kit.* Make up a simple one of your own, using some of the ideas as described later in this book.

how does a leader plan for a specific party?

The most successful party is one whose leader and planning committee have had a *sense of direction.* We say "and committee" because to draw several persons from the group, representing various interests and backgrounds, into a planning committee to work with the leader, is invaluable. Here are some of the questions the committee will ask itself as it sits down to plan for the event:

Who is likely to come? What ages are included? What kinds of recreation have they had during the past few months?

What do they like to do, and what don't they like to do?
(An interest finder that has been checked previously by members of the group will help to answer this question.)

What is the physical situation, such as size of room, equipment available, if any? If the affair is to be held outdoors, what are the circumstances? Place for swimming? Place for athletic contests? Any dangers to be guarded against for small children (if they are involved)?

How much time is available? This is important, for usually there is time for only about two-thirds as many activities as are planned. The best parties stop as well as begin on time. (Nevertheless, several "spares" available—games and leaders—may come in handy.)

Is this affair to be largely one of entertainment or of participation?

What are the goals for the group, toward which social affairs can help? Sociability? Getting acquainted? (If they are already acquainted, for instance, it is absurd to play get-acquainted games.) Self-expression and development of skills? Learning how to work together as a group? Hospitality to another group? Intercultural relationships? Developing appreciations? Developing group responsibility?

what are some general planning pointers?

Certain pointers or tips on recreation leadership hold good, no matter what type of social affair is held:

The use of imagination is rewarding. Try to make the event different, unusually interesting—don't just use the same worn-out ideas that have been used again and again.

Attention-catching publicity helps. Use the telephone, postal cards, novel posters, special mailings, personal contacts, mystery angles, such as "Burma Shave" signs. Get the newcomers out to the party by having them called for the first time by "old" members.

One person with final authority should be in charge. (Some social affairs are sloppy because no one person is responsible.) There can, however, be many assistants.

Drawing on members of the group itself for leadership of some of the activities is valuable. This is in keeping with the effort to develop self-confidence and leadership skills in the group.

Be sure that the attitude and standards of any "outside" leader whom you bring in occasionally for a change are in keeping with those of your organization. Otherwise, embarrassing or unfortunate situations may arise.

Something for firstcomers to do is desirable. (See Group Starters, page 57, for ideas.) Informal activities are suitable, such as singing around the piano, identifying objects on a table, swapping jokes, exchanging feats and tricks.

Providing special fun for the clean-uppers and returners of borrowed properties, and using amusing names for tasks to be done, are good psychology. (It won't be so difficult at the next party to get volunteers for these jobs!)

Public recognition of those who have made the event a success is a courteous and gracious gesture.

There are times for spontaneity. A good leader can sometimes "play the group by ear." Even though he has made careful preparations, he is sensitive to the mood of the group and can shift to another tune. For example, an active program has been planned, but everybody arrives exhausted after an unbearably hot, humid day. Try shifting, then, to quiet games, skits, riddles, or feats. "Can you do this?" you may ask the group, showing them a trick. Soon everyone will be eager to show off his favorite feat. Spontaneous group singing, joke telling, conundrums—all these can bring relaxation and give many people a chance to win recognition through sharing some personal accomplishment.

Reading aloud is a way of giving the group a chance to take it easy. Have available for impromptu use material like Colonel Stoopnagle's stories in *My Tale Is Twisted*, Bob

Benchley's short squibs, Stephen Leacock's nonsense, Roark Bradford's *Ol' Man Adam* tales, Richard Chase's mountain stories in *Grandfather Tales*. If children are present, material suitable for them can be used, too.

how is the planning for an event lined up?

Two sample plans for recreational events—for a picnic, and for a party—are blocked out below. The answers in parentheses are, of course, merely illustrative, and the questions serve only to suggest the kind of detailed thinking that the leader and his planning committee need to do in preparation for the event.

A PICNIC IS PLANNED

1. How many are coming? What kind of people? (About fifty or sixty. Whole families coming.)
2. Will they know each other? (Yes.)
3. Where can we go? (To the park out on the edge of town. There is a swimming pool, and a playground for the children.)
4. What about food? (Each family will bring assigned dishes; a committee will buy fruit, plan for drinks and refreshments.)
5. Publicity? (A telephone committee will follow up a postal card sent out. Also, announcements will be made at the group meetings.)
6. What games shall we play? (Our objective is to get families to play as families, so we'll have a number of games in which whole families can take part.)
7. When will they arrive? (About 6 o'clock. We'll have three helpers at the playground to be in charge of the children.)
8. What shall we do with the adults who arrive early? (We'll have Horseshoe Pitching, Washer Tossing, Volleyball, and we are rigging up a Goofy Golf game, using hockey sticks and rubber balls the size of golf balls,

knocked into tin cans around a "course." We have permission to put the cans in the ground.)

9. Who will be in charge of the meal? (A committee will set up the tables and spread the food. We will have a grace sung by everybody.)

10. Any contests? (Yes, on a family basis: Three-Legged Race for father and son, mother and daughter; Sack Races for both; Shoe-Kicking Contest by families—see who can kick shoe off the farthest; Discus Throw by families for distance—using paper plates; Javelin Throw, using soda straws.)

11. Doing anything near the water? (If there is time, we'll get the children to do some simple singing games in the water, parents participating.)

12. What about music? (We are having some group singing. The local band is performing that night, so we shall all go over near the bandstand after supper to enjoy the concert.)

A PARTY IS PLANNED

1. Where will it be? (Here at the hall.)

2. How many are coming? (Probably thirty.)

3. What have we done recently? (Frankly, not much—only a skating party and a family night in the past four months.)

4. Can we get an idea from the season of the year? (Let's have a Roundup Party, to start the program year off right this fall.)

5. What about decorations? (The committee will get some hay, and maybe combine decorations with the usual Hallowe'en sort of thing—minus cats.)

6. What about publicity? (We'll assign that to a committee of three. They are to make posters, give unusual announcements at meetings, hold a contest for the best singing commercial for the Roundup Party, telephone volunteers and prospective guests.)

7. Where can we look for ideas? (*The Fun Encyclopedia* would give some help. The program committee will work on this, too. "What do you do at a roundup?" Gather in the strays . . . we have some in the club. Do some roping and branding . . . we can do that—we have a fellow who can teach some of us to spin ropes. We could have that "Wild West Weakling" stunt from the back of *Skit Hits*. Storytelling around a "campfire" would be good, too.)

8. How do you see the program working out, then? (Here are the steps:

We'll go around and bring the members who haven't been coming.

When they first arrive, everybody will brand himself—by burning with a wood burner from craft supplies—a name tag, using a Western nickname.

We're changing an "oldie" game to "Pin the Rider on the Bronco." Each person is blindfolded, and turned around. He tries to pin the rider in the proper place on the bronco on the wall.

Next is the reading of "The Wild West Weakling" to get us in the mood. Everybody responds with noises of shots, Indians, coyotes, and the like.

Then comes a musical game or a square dance, either Texas Schottische or Texas Star, for which we have a caller.

Now comes a relay, with six players on each team. Each team has a lasso for the first player, who goes up to the goal twenty feet away and lassos a "calf" that we have made from a burlap sack filled with hay, and drags it back to his team. The next player drags it to the goal again by the rope, releases the rope, and comes back. First team through, wins.

15

Time now to rest up and play Scrambles, words from "roundups" and "ranchers" with the letters scrambled.

We have several active games to use in the middle for "spares."

Refreshments will be served from an imitation chuck wagon.

After that, there will be singing around the "campfire," which we'll build by lighting some candles in the center of the room and turning out all the lights.

2

a stockpile of ideas

fun in families

Here are some theme ideas for home fun for every member of the family and for interfamily entertainment, too. There are even some ideas for occasions when families can work together and yet have a lot of fun.

Badminton Party. Don't invite too many guests, but have enough that it will be fun to play badminton on the family court or lawn. Use other skill games, such as washer tossing or croquet golf. (For the latter, use croquet equipment but with holes in the ground. As in golf, try to knock the ball into the hole in the least number of strokes.)

Bottle Warmers Party. Two or three mothers who have young children get together for a morning visit while the babies sleep—they hope. They compare notes on feeding and on favorite recipes while they enjoy a cup of coffee and a bun.

"Children's Day." After Mother's Day and Father's Day celebrations are over, the family might set aside a "Children's Day" and be especially good to the children!

Chili Supper. Serving chili con carne is an easy way to entertain family friends.

Co-operative Dinner. Two families at a time are enough for this event. The hostess makes out the menu in advance, calling for simple dishes. When the guests arrive, each adult draws the name of one of the dishes to be prepared, and each child, the name of an adult to work with. Working thus in pairs, everybody has a part in preparing the meal, setting the table, and serving.

Crafteteria. Various odds and ends of craft materials—shells, bells, spools, cardboard tubing, foils, lollipops, felt, cork, leather, feathers, scraps of cloth, pipe cleaners, toothpicks, cards—are assembled on a table, and the guests make favors for the trays of hospital patients for Christmas.

Dessert Party. After each of the families have finished their first courses of a meal, they get together for dessert and games. (Select games from "Basic Half Dozens for Fun" and from "The Leader's Fun Kit" in this book.)

Dunworkin' Party. For the retired friends of the family or perhaps of grandpa or grandma. Some things to do: to tell one's most embarrassing experience, narrowest escape, most interesting recollection of one's life. Older folk too enjoy games like Spin the Bottle, Stop the Music, Sense of Smell, Hat Stunt. They like especially to sing.

Father's Day. Make a little extra fuss over dad. Cook his favorite food, give him some nice presents. For a surprise, invite some of his friends to drop in for the evening.

Fatties Anonymous. This affair is probably for mother or sister. They invite some of the "gals" who want to reduce, for one of those light lunches! In this way, they encourage each other.

Flashlight Party. Everybody is told to bring a flashlight. (1) Try signaling, using the Morse code of dots and dashes. (2) Play I Spy, using flashlights to find what is hidden. (3) Put a sheet up in the doorway, have a shadow play, using comic strip characters. (4) Have some special acts, using flashlights as spotlights.

Fried Chicken Party. Served indoors or outdoors, this hits the spot with everybody. Select games from "The Leader's Fun Kit" or "Basic Half Dozens for Fun."

Grill Party. Cooking and serving from an outdoor grill is always fun. Play some outdoor games found in "The Leader's Fun Kit."

Happy Birthday! Every family should have a celebration for every member when he has a birthday.

Hat Party. The women of the family invite other women

friends over and all make hats. This may take two or three sessions.

Hay Party (Slumber Party). The girls like to have a few of their friends in for a slumber party. For this one they are invited to "hit the hay." Have informal things for the girls to do, like making fudge in the kitchen or trying their hand at finger painting (get materials at art or school supply stores). Mostly they'll love to talk.

Home Movie (or Slides) Party. If you have a movie camera, invite another family to come with their reels of family pictures. They watch yours, you watch theirs. You might decide to make some movies together.

House (or Barn) Raising. Neighbors and friends, banded together, help a family build a temporary shack to live in if they have been burned out, or a place to store their crops. Or they help clean up and paint an old house the family has moved into. Games, jokes, singing, and refreshments along with the hard work can make fun out of it.

Kitchen Party. Mother invites a friend or two for lunch and together they "cook up" something. This is the time to try new recipes.

Lawnmowers Party. You come to my yard and help me mow, then I'll come over to yours and help you. Of course, some lemonade and a radio tuned on the ballgame go along with it.

Linoleum Party. This is for the little tots, who come and play on the linoleum (or rug). For the youngest, toys and refreshments are enough.

Magazine Party. Have a bunch of old magazines, scissors, and paste. Some activities like these might be fun: (1) See what it would cost a girl to keep her figure, her breath, her teeth, and her popularity, according to estimates in the ads. (2) Construct a play for radio or TV, using ads or stories or anything found in the magazines for a starter. (3) Read aloud jokes from the joke pages.

Merry-Go-Round Party. Gather up some of the neighbor-

19

hood children and take them to the park for rides and fun on the merry-go-round. If you take along balloons and your own refreshments, it's cheaper than buying them there. Have enough adults or young people along to supervise the little tots.

Mother's Day. Let the family take over, prepare the meal, and invite some of mother's favorite friends for the day. Have a lot of small presents for her. If the invited guests are mothers, they too could be honored.

Moving Party. When a family is moving, get several neighbors together and help it out, cook its noon meal, and so on. The family leaves that neighborhood, then, with a good feeling.

On Location Party. With a movie camera and a short script, actually make a movie, with some invited friends present. This might take more than one session. Assign jobs to each person such as script girl, sound or camera man, properties, makeup, and so on.

Pat-a-Cake. This is for the younger set. They invite friends in to make a cake or other goodies in the kitchen.

Pet Party. Hold a pet show, getting all the invited children to bring their pets. Let each pet do tricks. Serve "dogs" or "hay" (frankfurters or Shredded Wheat).

Pickup Party. A family which owns a truck sends the truck around to pick up all the invited youngsters, bringing them back to the farm or ranch for a coke party, a rodeo, barbecue, or swimming party.

Pop's Concert. If dad happens to be musical, invite some of his friends for an evening program of good records or for a special radio program. Or the theme might be music by certain composers or certain conductors. Let the youngsters go out on this occasion unless they too will listen quietly.

Skinnies Anonymous. The party is just like Fatties Anonymous, but this crowd tries to eat as much as possible.

Tape Recorders Party. Everybody likes to perform. Invite other families in to record on tape and hear their voices back, or let the group put on a skit and record it (see *The Handbook of Skits and Stunts* for ideas). Send the tape to mutual friends far away or to boys in the service.

TV Party. For young or old—invite guests for particular television shows that are good. Or, divide guests (and your own family) into two or three groups and let them put on a "TV" program, using a doorway as your TV screen. Hold a TV quiz, too.

Textile Stenciling. This makes a nice party for the older boys and girls and adults. Men enjoy this craft as well as women, once they get started. This is a good time to make Christmas presents.

Trick and Magic Party. If you know someone who does magic, ask him to perform when you invite some friends in for a magic party. Perhaps he will let you in on the secret of a trick or two. (See *The Fun Encyclopedia* for some tricks.)

Vacation Party. After families have returned from their vacations, let those who know each other well bring over their pictures and souvenirs some evening and have a big time.

Wolf Party. The girls get together and invite their favorite "wolves," either separately or in droves. They play games like Truth or Consequences, Spin the Bottle, Suitcase Relay, Balloon Volleyball, one-word stunts.

fun in other groups

Thus far we have been talking about all kinds of fun that the family can have by itself or with other families. Now let's see what kinds of activities can give a group outside the home a good time.

OUTDOORS AND AWAY

Baseball (Basketball or Football) Party. Get together, go to the game, whoop it up. Also to movies (another time).

Beeline Hike. Get together in a woodsy spot, then use a compass and go straight ahead on a beeline, veering away only to go around trees, across bridges over streams, and the like.

Bowling Ball. Get the crowd together at one place and waltz down to the bowling alley. Alleys usually need to be rented in advance. Offer prizes for the lowest and the highest scores, and for the one who tried the hardest. Return to the meeting place for refreshments.

Chinatown Venture. If you live in or near a city that has a Chinatown, make a trip there for a meal and for browsing through the stores. Your group might arrange with a somewhat similar group of Chinese background for a joint meeting. Exchange games. (You may find their games similar to yours!) Take flash pictures and use them later to describe the trip.

Color Tour. In spring and fall, many thoughtful groups get out their cars and invite shut-ins to go on a color tour.

Crazy Critter Hike. One resourceful recreation leader gets groups to look for nature objects that can be interpreted as animals, or people. Rocks, pieces of bark, roots, unusual nature growths, limbs and branches (on the ground, of course) furnish food for the imagination. Moss, nuts, toadstools may be picked to put eyes, hair, ears on these Crazy Critters. When you get back, have a display. (This is a good camp activity.)

H_2O Party. This is a swimming party by another name. Have fun swimming, but also play water games. Folk games in the water are enjoyable, also Dodge Ball, Keep Away (divide into two teams using a floating rubber ball and try to keep it away from opponents); Tug of War in the water; Candle Relay (you must take lighted candle up to goal and back, give to next person in line, until all on your side have gone; if candle goes out, you must return to light it). Other land games can be adapted.

Moonlight Hike. After dark, equipped with flashlights, go on a mellow moonlight hike. At the end, make a campfire, cook a meal or have refreshments, and sing. Tell ghost stories.

Pedal Pushers Shindig. Have a bike party, and make a trip to some chosen spot, or just start out on a "Random Skoot." To combine the bike trip with a swimming party is fun, too.

Penny Walk. In the city, for a diversion, divide into several small groups, each with a leader and a penny. At each intersection, flip the penny: if heads, go to the left, if tails, go to the right. Return to the starting place by a given time, for refreshments, telling of adventures, and singing.

Possum Hunt. It's fun to have an imitation possum or two placed in trees in advance. The group goes out into the woods at night to try to find them. Give some clues, if necessary.

Speedboat Party (or other boat trip). Make up a party to go to some place on a lake where speedboat rides are sold. Better, hire a larger boat for a party. Many games and stunts in "The Leader's Fun Kit" section or "Basic Half Dozens for Fun" are appropriate. Sing a lot.

Studio TV. Many television studios want an audience. Get your crowd together and go, or be a radio audience.

Treasure Hunt. The course must be laid out in advance. Clues in rhyme are good. Divide the larger group into smaller hunting groups. When they find a paper containing a clue, they read it, then put it back. "First my trusty horse I'm mounting, then I'm looking by the fountain." (There at the fountain they will find another clue.) Plan carefully so that the clues actually lead to the treasure (which may be the supper, to be cooked outdoors, or it could be milk chocolate gold pieces, available at many candy stores).

Watermelon Party. Many groups have a watermelon cuttin', either to raise money or just to have fun. How about "stealing" watermelons? Have them hidden in a field, with a group, the "farmers," ready to defend the patch. Another group tries to spirit some melons away. After the fun, everybody gathers to eat the watermelons and to play games such as Seed Squirt (squeeze the seeds and make them jump). Hold a contest for the best set of false teeth made from the rind or for the most unusual craftsmanship in carving rinds. (Don't forget to take knives along.)

Here are some parties at which some person is specially honored or some occasion is specially observed within a group.

Baby Shower. Honor the mamas-to-be. Besides giving gifts for the little one, gather up baby pictures of guests, and guess who is who. Have a contest to name the baby. Put on a skit showing how mother will act when she gets home from the hospital.

Back to the Salt Mines. This party is fun for any group who have had time off and are now to return to the job. One group used the occasion to show what the reactions would be back home if they tried to put into practice improvements and ideas which they had just learned at the summer conference.

Birthday Observances. Many groups include, in their regular program, special recognition of birthdays, with speeches, presents, and donations of money, by the ones honored, to the group's treasury.

Cat and Kitten Party. This is a mother-daughter banquet or party idea. After a good meal, toasts are offered to the mother-daughter combinations. Ask them in advance to come prepared to perform with music, speeches, poetry, or jokes. Hold a quiz, with mothers on one side, daughters on the other. Get each group to sing to the other.

Come Double Party. This party is especially for couples. Have lots of fun, music, games, and laughter. There are many suitable games in the Kit and Basic Half Dozens.

Dad and Lad Party. For a father-son banquet or party use the same ideas as described in the Cat and Kitten Party above.

Going to College Party. Honor those who are going off to college for past service in the club. Present in skit form what they are going to meet at college. Take up with much exaggeration classroom life, social life, athletics, roommate, and so on, and in the skit show them meeting their future mates.

Music Memories. Honoring someone who has rendered long service, weave a story using song titles to bring back to their memories incidents of the past.

This Is Your Life. Unknown to the person honored, get in advance some scenes from his past life, and act them out for him. These might be followed with the presentation of a gift, medal, or some other recognition.

WORK PARTIES

Just as families find they can have fun when they do a hard job together, other groups find it possible, too.

Artists Party. When a coming event in the organization needs to be publicized, hold a sign- or poster-painting spree.

Bag Party. The "bags" (girls) bring flour sacks or other cloth and make aprons, dresses, and the like.

Canning Bee. Those who are going to can, all get together at one spot for mutual assistance. They may can for an organization (like the Hot Lunch Committee of the PTA) or for themselves, dividing the cost.

Floor-Sanding Party. In refinishing the meeting room, usually the boy friends and husbands will do this. Girls or women serve refreshments to the big, strong fellows.

Harvest Party or Festival. This could be a go-to-the-fields affair, with everyone helping. See who harvests the most. Sing as you work. Hold a worship service at the end in celebration of the harvest.

KP Party. This is a special party for the clean-up crew after the big party is over. Let them draw lots for slips that have letters like "DD" (dry dishes), "SF" (sweep floor), indicating which job they are to do. Save out some extra refreshments for them.

Painting Party. Your group might get together and paint the home of one of its members, or perhaps the church, lodge,

25

school or community building. Singing and refreshments lend fun.

Sewing Circle. The "gals" get together and make something, preferably for someone else—for example, mending clothes for relief groups.

Slave Party. Members volunteer their services to be bought for window washing, lawn mowing, brush clearing. Have refreshments for the group at the end of the work day.

Toy Patch Party. Round up old toys for the group to repair. This project might need two or three sessions.

Tree Planting. Some groups make this an annual affair, especially at camps. Part of the fun comes twenty years later when your tree is a big one.

Typewriter (or Mimeographing) Party. An organization has a lot of appeals or reports to get out. Round up volunteers for this job and serve refreshments.

Waste Paper Party. Gather paper for the organization to sell, then play games that can be done with newspapers. Make costumes, play Swat, have a newspaper relay.

GENERAL PARTIES

Adam and Eve Party. Come in bathing suits or wearing them underneath street clothes. Play games as they might have been in the Garden of Eden; for instance, instead of Spin the Bottle, spin a banana. Play games with whole coconuts, such as passing games. Then crack the coconuts and eat later as part of the refreshments. This is an outdoor party idea.

Battle of the Sexes. This is almost the same as the Turnabout Party below, but out to prove which is the superior sex. Keep scores rigidly. Have quizzes, relays, competitive games. At the end, get a male to admit that the females are superior, and vice versa, just to keep things interesting!

Book Swappers Party. (Phonograph records could be swapped as well.)

Kid Party. Everyone dresses like a kid and acts like one. Sing "School Days." Plày kid games and otherwise act kiddish.

Kodachrome Party. People with 35 mm. cameras come to make slides, then show them at a later meeting. Use a script and photograph a story.

March of Time Party. Choose several sample years and plan events in keeping with the period: for instance A.D. 1, 1492, 1776, 1940. Skits could show the manner of food preparation, taking a bath, courting, and the like. Larger crowds could be divided into smaller groups to work up these skits. Some could be planned ahead, photographed on slides, and shown with running commentary.

Pancake Supper (or Fish Fry). One group (perhaps the men) prepares the supper; the women come to eat and enjoy it. This could also be a money-raising idea.

School Daze Party. For decorations, imitate the Little Red Schoolhouse that almost nobody goes to anymore, and have readin', writin', and 'rithmetic, when the school board comes to visit—all acted out. Recitations could be done in quiz form, with classes divided into halves, competing. Music could be by individual performers or by the group. At "recess," play active games. Hand out lunch boxes for refreshments, having asked each guest in advance to bring his own.

Shoe Party. One group held a shoe party, gathering up old shoes from all those attending, and sent them off for overseas relief. They played games involving shoes like Shoe Scramble (all take off shoes, scramble them in the middle of the floor, see who can find his pair first and put them on properly laced), Pass This Shoe, and other games suggested in *The Fun Encyclopedia.*

Turnabout Party. The boys come as girls, the girls as boys. The girls ask the boys for dates. In games roles are reversed. Skits are takeoffs on the other sex. Males sing female numbers in falsetto voices, girls sing as low as they can. Boys prepare and serve the refreshments.

Circus. More groups should put on an amateur circus for fun. Have a ringmaster, a parade, animals, sideshows, barkers, and all the rest. The affair can even be done "spontaneously" if a committee working in advance will bring materials for a "band," for animals (blankets, butcher paper, pins, large paper sacks, brooms, Crayolas or showcard colors), costume material for the ringmaster, properties for the sideshows. Divide the crowd into small work groups, with an assignment for which they are allowed fifteen to thirty minutes, then let them put on their various acts. Some acts may not be so good, but many will be very well done.

Country Store. The stage is arranged like an old country store. Skits are held there and games are conducted by the storekeeper. Refreshments are served from a shelf or from behind the counter.

Folk Festival. Hold a festival, using fun ideas from different countries, including songs, games, stories, perhaps foods. If there are folk of other nationality background in your community, draw them in to take part. Plan to have in some parts of the program events that most of the group can watch and in other parts the kind of activities that they can enter into, such as simple folk songs and games. Some suggestions are found in *And Promenade All,* and in *Folk Party Fun.*

Good Earth Festival. This would be a harvest festival, bringing in the fruits of the season, with thanksgiving to God for his bounty. The occasion should be fun, but would probably strike a serious note, too. The program might consist of a good supper, singing around the table, a reading of appropriate psalms, a thanksgiving prayer. Joyful folk games would be fitting. (See *And Promenade All.*)

Hobby Show. Get the members of the group to bring their hobby materials to the meeting place for a big hobby show. Each hobbyist tells about his particular interest. Have a general session, a "Hobby Lobby," in which people may

28

"lobby" (Washington style) for hobbies. Perhaps a drama group could put on a play or skit. Music hobbyists could perform.

Life at the Office (or Plant, Church, Club, or School). This is a setting for many stunts and dramatizations of the lunch hour, office, school classroom or of the bosses. Give a skit on "How the Other Half Lives."

Stock Show. After the group arrives, give them some atmosphere music and a stunt or two, such as "Old McDonald Had a Farm" and "He Ain't Done Right by Nell" in *The Handbook of Skits and Stunts.* Divide the crowd into small groups, each of which is to enter an "animal" in the show. Have some of the "animals" perform tricks in front of the judging team.

Stop the Music. In a musical program, of which this would be just one feature, play Stop the Music. As the record, piano, or organ plays, someone will recognize the composition or the song and will say "Stop the music!" and tries to identify it correctly. If he is correct he gets a candy kiss.

Storytellers Convention. Here is a quieter kind of activity which uses the skill of storytellers. Libraries are full of good stories and tall tales. See also "References," page 63.

Stunt Night. Organizations that have departments, classes, or floors find it good fun to ask each unit to work up a stunt or two for a stunt night. A master of ceremonies will be needed and perhaps some committees for publicity, refreshments, staging. There could be music and readings in addition to stunts.

skits and stunts

ONE- OR TWO-WORD STARTERS

Most groups enjoy seeing skits, and many people enjoy being in them. Here is a list of words and names to use as idea starters if you want to get the group to create its own stunts or skits. Divide a large group into small ones and assign one of the idea starters below to each group, to set their thoughts in motion. Allow ten to fifteen minutes, or longer if there is time, for the groups to work up a skit from their assignments.

Illustration: "7. Kidnapped." Home scene, beautiful girl inside. Thugs pass by the window, like her looks. As they sneak into the house, homely aunt takes the girl's chair, unseen by thugs. They kidnap her, throwing something over her head. When they get her outside and throw off the covering they screech and let her go!

1. Embarrassed	18. Hidden	35. Secret passage
2. Mortgage	19. Rural	36. Lost colony
3. Wreck	20. Shot	37. Napoleon
4. Mystery	21. Sinking	38. George Washington
5. Gun	22. Body	ton
6. Missing	23. Lights out	39. Alexander the
7. Kidnapped	24. Space men	Great
8. Speechless	25. Sinking	40. Helen of Troy
9. Mistaken	26. Hi-jackers	41. Queen of Sheba
10. Scream	27. Tornado	42. Underworld king
11. Falling	28. South Seas	43. Queen Elizabeth
12. Crash	29. Stiletto	44. Sir Walter
13. Alarm	30. Killer loose	Raleigh
14. Innocent	31. Alarm broadcast	45. Pocahontas
15. Sale	32. Pirate chest	46. John Paul Jones
16. Explosion	33. Hidden gold	47. Caesar
17. Disappeared	34. Amnesia victim	48. Little Abner

SOME SKIT SITUATIONS

These situations are given briefly to stimulate your imagination. If you need more help in completing skits and stunts, see *The Handbook of Skits and Stunts*. Some of the ones which follow may be old to you, some new.

A la Spike Jones. Have one group or several choose a song and present it the way Spike Jones might do it.

Bargain Counter. Ladies are shopping. Timid man waits

patiently for a long time, finally lowers head, and charges straight up to counter. "Sir, why don't you act like a gentleman?" asks a horrified woman. "That's what I was doing," he replies, "and now I'm acting like a lady."

Bird Courtship. This skit takes some work, but can be fun. Two fellows, dressed like a male and a female bird with feathers and wings, carry on a courtship with chirps, clucks, motions, wing flapping. He makes advances, she declines. Finally he offers a ring. She chirps yes.

Chef. He prides himself on inspecting all food leaving kitchen, the chef tells visitor. Kitchen helper passes by with large soup container. "Wait, let me taste that!" the chef orders. The helper shakes his head no and starts to say, "But . . ." "Not a word," says the chef—then he spews it out, exclaiming, "That tastes like dishwater!" "I was trying to tell you, sir. That's what it is!"

George and the Dragon. A tramp knocks at the door of an English inn, plainly labeled "George and the Dragon." When he asks for a bite to eat, woman screams "No!" at him unpleasantly, slams door. He knocks again. She opens door, starts to say something violently, but he cuts in quickly, "Now, could I have a few words with George?"

George Rides Again. A group of people are on the train. One claims he is George Washington. They all scoff. Conductor calls out, "Mount Vernon!" "George" gets up, says it's his station, and gets off. They all look at one another uncertainly.

Lie Detector. Have a "lie detector machine" which rings bells, turns on lights, makes noises when a person tells a lie. Call up several well-known persons, ask them test questions. Machine is operated by persons out of sight, of course.

Living Pictures. Describe a life situation and then pull the curtain, behind which is a "picture," acted out by real people. The situation could be humorous or serious.

Lost Sheep. After an elaborate build-up by the announcer of the song "The Lost Sheep," including an introduction of operatic nature on the piano, the singer goes, "Baaaaa!"

Mother Goose. Any of the Mother Goose rhymes lend themselves to dramatization.

One in a Thousand. To show Solomon's wisdom, present this short sketch. One of the girls is with Solomon—who is bathrobed, to imitate the costume of his day—and says, "Sol, do you really, really love me?" "My dear," says Solomon, "You are one in a thousand." "Oh, Sol!" she cries, snuggling closer.

Operation. This is a shadow stunt. Hang a sheet in a doorway, put a strong light behind it, and operate on a victim on a table placed against the sheet on side away from audience. The doctors remove a half-inflated balloon for a lung, and take out strings of weiners and a cardboard heart (held close to sheet). One assistant takes out a tin can, saying, "Here it is, doctor—a can, sir!"

Paul Revere's Ride. Paul Revere makes elaborate preparations, including lanterns, and so forth. Rides stick horse up to one house after another, crying, "The British are coming!" At one door a beautiful girl steps out. Revere takes a look, ties his horse, and is evidently stopping there. "To heck with the British!" says Paul.

Style Show. Men take the roles of women. This is always fun.

Sunday School. The teacher is trying to teach the lesson. "What were the Philistines killed with by Sampson?" None of the children know. Finally she gives a hint, touching her face. "What's this?" "Oh, I know," exclaims a bright child. "The jawbone of an ass!"

Teachin' Him to Swim. A man is warned not to fish without a license. He goes anyway, and is fishing, perhaps over edge of stage. Hears steps behind him. "You the game warden?" "Yep." Man points to worm on end of hook." Jest teachin' him to swim."

Telephone Scene. A person tries to use the phone, but cannot get a local number through. Several people call world points from the same pay telephone. Finally he calls a distant friend, gets him to relay a message to his wife down the street.

Too Many Suitors (an oldtimer, but good for a laugh). The girl has many callers, one at a time. They bring presents. When the second one knocks, she makes the first one into a chair by having him kneel and throwing a blanket over him. Likewise she creates from the other suitors hatracks, divans, tables, and the like. Finally a later caller tries to sit on the divan. All tumble over and run out. Consternation!

Trial. Accuse a member of the group of some humorous charge, have a jury, lawyers, defendants, witnesses, and judge.

Wishing Well. People bend over an improvised well, ask it questions. It answers back, the echo being a witty person who can "ad lib." "O wishing well, O wishing well," each one is supposed to say—then give his wish. One person wishes he had a million dollars, and the well replies "So-o-o-o do-o-o-o I-i-i-i!"

CAN YOU DO THIS?

The following stunts for informal times are suitable for a small group that is "loafing" or waiting, and yet they can be used in an organized social affair too, some of them as contests. Many of them involve co-ordination. Once any of these are started, the group thinks of others quickly. Can you . . .

1. Write with both hands at the same time?
2. Recite the alphabet backwards? (As a gag, turn backwards and recite it in the regular order.)
3. Describe a spiral staircase without using your hands?
4. Pat your head, rub your tummy at same time?
5. Make a circular motion with jaw, figure 8 with head, at same time?
6. Balance a yardstick on your finger?
7. Wiggle scalp without wiggling ears?
8. Touch your wrist with your thumb?
9. Jump in air, feet straight in front of you parallel to ground or floor, touch toes?

10. Whistle the longest in one breath?
11. Eat a cracker and be the first to whistle?
12. Give the incorrect answer quickly to questions that can be answered yes or no? (For example: "George Washington was the first president." "No.")
13. Blindfolded, blow out a candle in three blows?
14. Blindfolded, tell someone's identity by feeling face only?
15. Act out a word so that the group gets it in two minutes or less?
16. Hold the most water cupped in your two hands?
17. Swing a filled pail over head without spilling water?
18. With a figure 8 motion, turn a plate under arm and over head, and right it without spilling contents or dropping plate?
19. Flip the cork? (Place cork on top of a soft-drink bottle, on edge of table. Walk by, arm straight in front of you, flip cork without slowing down.)
20. Make an eight-sided salt shaker stand on edge? (It is possible. Shake a little salt on table, set one side of base in the salt at a 45-degree angle to table. Experimentation will allow shaker to stand on edge unassisted.)
21. Drop a penny into a small glass at bottom of a water-filled jar?
22. Kneel, grasp insteps with hands, walk on knees?
23. Lie on back, fold arms on chest, then stand, arms still folded?
24. With heels touching wall, bend over and pick up a handkerchief?
25. Say any of these tongue twisters three times in rapid succession without a mistake:
    a. She sells sea shells at the seashore.
    b. Six thick thistles stick.
    c. Quizzical quiz, kiss me quick.
    d. Theophilus Thistle the thistle sifter thrust three thousand thistles through the thick of his thumb.
    e. The sea ceaseth and it sufficeth us.

f. Sister Susie swiftly sewed sixty shirts for seventy sailors.

g. Ziggy Jazinsky slurped his soup.

h. Three gray geese on three green hills.

i. Peter Piper picked a peck of pickled peppers.

music for fun

A FEW TIPS ON SONG LEADING

The good song leader does not necessarily know all there is to be known about music. In fact, there are some song leaders who cannot even carry a tune; they depend on the piano for the tune and they guide the rhythm. If you are to lead the singing, check these points for help:

1. Whatever you do, remember that you are helping people to have fun in singing.
2. Sing with the group and enjoy doing it.
3. Remember the reasons for having a leader—to give the pitch, to set the tempo, and to interpret, sometimes to teach the song.
4. In teaching, break up the song into small bits that can be learned easily.

WHEN MUSIC IS USED

Practically every group likes to sing, and all groups like to hear music performed. Every well-balanced fun program will include some music. Here are suggestions for the use of music:

Look for interesting settings for singing—down by the lake, up close around the piano, around the campfire.

Choose music appropriate for the occasion.

Select a good songbook for use in the group.[1]

For group singing, use songs that are either familiar or easily taught.

---

[1] There are many folksong collections available from Co-operative Recreation Service, Delaware, Ohio.

Include some lively songs, action songs.[2]

Let music create moods. This can be done by careful choice of the songs to be rendered by performers or by the group, for instance, quiet songs, hymns, spirituals.

Before a meal, a grace sung by the whole group is appropriate.

Give a concert, using either group talent or professional talent. A city-wide youth group presented Roland Hayes in concert with significant results.

Put on a musical show, using the talent of the group.

Amateur Night settings are always fun. Use a microphone or improvised television camera for additional color.

Have an Old Times Narration, recalling in song the things of yesteryear. An old couple on the stage might carry on conversation indicating memories of days gone by.

Give the music a setting. Have a Cowboy Quartet, Policemen's Trio, or the like.

Acting out songs makes a good program item.

Song themes, such as work songs, heart songs, and so on, help to organize a program.

Play "Stop the Music." When one of the audience recognizes the tune, he calls out, "Stop the music!", then tries to identify it. If he is right he gets a point for his side or a small prize.

Have a connected story, using titles of songs. The songs are played, and the group asked to identify them. Here's a starter: He met her "Down in the Valley," "In the Evening by the Moonlight." He said, "Oh, in the Moonlight I Want to Hold Somebody's Hand. . . ."

Make up a story, using musical terms: sharp, flat, bar, brace, note, space, tremolo, accent, and so on.

Use phonograph records during the interims for meetings, banquets.

Make recordings of the musical presentation your group is giving on tape or disc.

Outdoors the campfire is a wonderful music organizer.

Indoors, to give the effect of a campfire, darken the room

---

[2] Interesting collection: *Camp Songs 'n' Things,* Wes Klusman, 1925 Addison, Berkeley, Calif., 25 cents.

and light several candles, close together. The flicker of the flame is more realistic than red bulbs.

Start-a-song. As a group sits informally, let someone start a song, asking others to join in. Then let someone else start one. This is especially good at campfires or in a darkened room.

Close a program with appropriate music—sometimes patriotic, sometimes with hymns and spirituals, if a church group.

Some groups enjoy using a fellowship circle at the very end of the occasion.

money raising and fun

Many groups need to raise money and have fun at the same time. This is perfectly possible, for the fellowship and unity of purpose are present, and so too are the other elements of good fun. Check through these ideas for some practical ones for your group.

Auction. Ask members to bring articles to be auctioned off.

Baby Sitting Service. Get members to donate their time and service at baby sitting, charging the regular rate for it.

Bake Sale. Members bake pies, cake, cookies, or rolls for a sale held in a location convenient to shoppers.

Beauty Party. Let the girls get together and work on each other, giving into the club treasury what they would have paid a beauty parlor.

Birthday Pay. Hold a social affair for which you charge by birthdays. (If this works a hardship on older folk, scale it down to a certain amount for those over fifty.)

Boat Rental. Hire an excursion boat, take a trip, and play interesting games on deck along the way.

Bowling. Rent an alley. Charge the members proportionately more than the rental cost.

Breakfast. Serve a special breakfast meal, perhaps using donated foods. The proceeds, of course, go to the group.

Breakfast in Bed Club. All who join must pay a fee. Two members of the group will come over to your house and serve your breakfast in bed.

Box Social. The girls fill the boxes with refreshments, the boys buy the boxes at auction.

Circus. Put this on, involving many people, and many more will come and pay to see the acts and the "big top."

Concert. Charge a fee for one with outstanding artists.

Copper Carnival. It costs a copper penny to participate in each attraction. Have many skill games like Bean Bag Tossing, Rubber Heel Tossing, Flip the Cork (3 tries for a penny); bounce ball over chair back into wastebasket (3 tries for a penny), toss jar rubbers onto hooks on a board (5 tries for a penny). Have small prizes. For sideshows, try these: Legless, Hairless Dog (wiener); The Fat Lady (girl—maybe a man—stuffed with pillows); Water Color Exhibition (20 glasses of water, each colored a different shade); For Men Only (razor and shaving brush); For Women Only (nail polish); Have Your Palm Read (the "fortune teller" puts mercurochrome in middle of palm). See *The Handbook of Skits and Stunts* for other suggestions.

County Fair or Carnival. Put on one, charge admission for sideshows, displays. Give donated prizes.

Coupon Collection. Some commercial firms will redeem coupons now, if gathered by large groups.

Crafteteria. Make small craft items to sell as party favors or decorations or for other purposes, using plastics, glass etching, raffia, or tin cans. Making winter flower corsages and quilting are profitable, too.

Excursion. Hire a bus or train to go to some outstanding affair, sell tickets at a profit. Have games planned to use on the way.

Fish Fry. Many groups raise money by serving a fish fry or other traditional meal annually. Be sure to plan for some fun in program form.

Folk Festival. Have songs, games, stories, and food of other nationalities, and charge admission.

Flower Show. Sponsor one, letting your group's financial needs be known.

Football Party. An excellent one is described in *The End of Your Stunt Hunt.* Put it on and charge a refreshment fee.

Ice Cream Party. Get members to bring homemade ice cream and cakes for sale. Or, better yet, freeze the ice cream on the spot.

Kitchen Party. (For girls, mostly.) Let anyone come, bringing their own ingredients, make their pet recipe, then sell what they have made.

Making and Selling Candles. Use scrap candles, mold in cardboard square milk cartons.[3]

Making and Selling Equipment Games. Descriptions can be found in most social recreation books.[4]

Pancake Supper. Some distributors will serve these without cost to the group. Charge for the supper. Or, make your own pancakes and charge admission.

Picture Show. Take movies of members, show later, and take up a collection.

Play. Putting on a play takes work, but it is fun all the way around. (See "References," page 64, for play publishers.)

Pop Stand. Get a concession for a pop stand, the profit for the group treasury.

Roving Photographer. Get someone with a flash camera to take pictures at group meetings, sell them to members at a profit for the group.

Rummage Sale. No explanation necessary—almost entirely clear profit!

Seed Dollar Plan. Give each member one dollar out of the group treasury, with which he is to do something which will earn more money for the group. Give a prize to the one who earns the most from his dollar investment and for the one whose method of earning is the most novel.

---

[3] Instructions and materials can be secured from Consumers Youth Department, 318 East 10th Street, Kansas City, Mo.

[4] Descriptive kits can be obtained also from Co-operative Recreation Service, Delaware, Ohio, at 25 cents.

Selling Books or Taking Magazine Subscriptions. The commission goes to the group treasury.

Sewing Class. Hold a sewing class with the understanding that the articles made in it will be sold for the group.

Skating. Rent a skating rink (ice or roller), charging members proportionately more than the rental costs.

Slave System. Members contribute to the group their services for a day or a half day, perhaps on a Saturday. People may bid for a "slave," then get him or her to wash, iron, put up screens, mow lawn, or whatever needs to be done.

Specialty Items. Get a specialty salesman's magazine, find articles there to sell on commission.

Stunt Night. Get each class, department, or floor to put on a Stunt Night. Pass the hat and serve refreshments.

Swimming Pool. Rent one and charge members proportionately more than the rental cost.

Starvation Banquet. Serve a very light meal, provide a program of entertainment, charge the price of a full dinner, and send the money to some overseas relief organization like Meals for Millions, 648 South Broadway, Los Angeles (a nonsectarian and nonprofit agency, distributing food at 3 cents a meal).

Television Parties in Homes. Arrange for homes to have simultaneous television parties. Each host or hostess takes up a collection.

Watermelon Cuttin'. This is a tasty way to make money.

Note: If a group charges admission it is subject to a 10 per cent Federal tax.

All groups subject to tax are supposed to pay it. All admissions are subject to tax, except as follows:

The newer provisions in the law state that a church, school or Community Chest group and the like operating on a nonprofit basis and using their income from admissions for educational and charitable purposes may apply for a tax exemption form 755 from their District Director of Internal Revenue.

This permission must be cleared before the event, else **tax** must be charged and collected.

Collections are better, or contributions made to the group treasury. If there is doubt as to what is required, it would be well to check with the Internal Revenue Department.

refreshment suggestions

Refreshments have a tendency to run in the same monotonous channels, but they do not have to do so. Much variety is possible, not only in content but in form, if imagination is used, as in some of these suggestions:

SANDWICHES AND OTHER FILLERS

Carrot sticks, celery
Chili con carne, crackers
Cold plate
Cornbread and beans (Hard Times Party, Hobo Hike)
"Dagwood" sandwiches (make your own)
Deviled eggs
Hamburgers (make your own)
"Hay" (Shredded Wheat)
Hot dogs (prepared, or make your own)
Outdoor corn roast
Peanuts (use "Pass the Peanuts" game: while music is played they are passed around the circle in a bowl. When music stops, whoever holds bowl may eat until music starts again)
Popcorn
Potato chips
Prepared sandwiches
Smörgasbord (assorted cold cuts, fish, cheese, relishes on a central table)
Steak fry
Weiner roast

FRUITS

Apples
Apple Santa Claus (using cotton, marshmallow head)
Baked apples
Bananas
Fruit salad
Grapes
Oranges
Orange or grapefruit, broiled
Peach face (eyes, nose, made of cloves)
Raisins
Stewed prunes, figs

Cakes
Candies
Candy bars
Candy pull
Canteloupe (with ice cream)
Coconut (let the group crack them, drink the milk, eat the meat)
Cookies
Crackers (get 5-cent packages for each guest)
Fudge (make it while they wait)
Jello (plain, molded, fruit in it)
Ice cream (try unusual molds)
Marshmallows, toasted (or make marshmallow turtles with raisins, cloves)
Orange juice milkshake (use 6-oz. glass of orange juice, vanilla ice cream, milk)
Pies
Popcorn balls
S'mores (put toasted marshmallow and chocolate bar square between graham crackers)
Strawberries
Suckers (for kids or kid parties)
Sundaes
Watermelon

It would be fun for the group to see firsthand how certain foods are made—for instance, visit an ice cream factory, "dairy freeze," or doughnut shop. Everybody goes!

DRINKS

Chocolate, hot
Cider
Coffee
Fruit punch
Kickapoo Joy Juice (regular, hi-test—amber or red lemonade with ginger ale added)
Kool Aid
Lemonade (plain, colored)
Milk (plain, slim skim, chocolate, buttermilk)
Milkshakes
Orange juice, other fruit juices
Root beer and pretzels
Soft drinks of all kinds
Tea, hot or iced

3

the leader's fun kit

Even though a person may only occasionally be called upon to be responsible for the games or recreational events of a group, he will find it useful to keep together in one place—perhaps in an old suitcase—many of the items listed below, each of which can be used over and over for many recreational purposes. A person doing a lot of leading would, of course, build up a much more elaborate and comprehensive kit of "properties." The following list is intended to be the items which might go into a "kit," but it suggests also games which can be played with these articles.

Accompaniment Books. For group singing.

Advertising Slogans. A list of slogans drawn from ads in magazines and newspapers or heard on radio, seen on TV. You read one slogan at a time from your list; members of the group call out the name of the firm.

Alphabet Spaghetti. Use for (a) spelling games, anagrams; (b) name tags, by pasting letters on cards.

Animal Heads, Tails. Pre-made—for skits, circuses.

Ball, 6″ in Diameter. (a) Batless baseball: Strike ball with hand when batting, otherwise play just as in softball. (b) Dodgeball: One or more players are in center of circle. Those in outer circle try to hit them with ball. (c) Keep Away: A team tries to keep the ball away from another team, either on land or in the water. (d) Safety Zone Ball: Excellent game for large groups, 25 on a side. (See *The Fun Encyclopedia* for rules.)

Ball, 10″ in Diameter. (a) Use for volley ball. (b) **Stride**

Ball: Players stand in circle, feet apart to form stride 18 inches wide. Center player tries to roll ball out under stride. Loser goes to center. (You may not move your feet.)

Balloons. (a) Balloon Volleyball: Play as in regular volleyball. Sometimes this can be played indoors with players seated. They try to knock balloon over a string which represents net. (b) Ball and Chain: Tie balloons to ankles of all. Each person tries to defend his own but burst that of another. (c) Swat Tail: Tie balloon on rear of each player, give each player rolled up newspaper. Each tries to defend his own balloon but burst others'. If his balloon collapses he is out. (d) Relay game: Run from your position to a chair placed ahead of your line, blow up balloon, burst it by sitting on it, run back to your line again. Several lines of six players each are simultaneously in competition.

Barnyard Din. Have paper squares of four colors to spread around the room. Each color is assigned to an animal, and each person to a color. Each color has a leader who is the only one who can come to pick up that bit of color. Players stand over the color when they find a square, giving the animal noise: cow, dog, rooster, and so on. (The game is also played with peanuts. Whoever finds one calls for his captain in this manner.)

Baton. For tricks.

Beanbags. (a) Beanbag Basketball: Human goal holds wastebasket at each end of court. The game is played as in basketball, except that it is all passing. "Goal" may move any part of the body except the feet, to help beanbag go in. (b) Use beanbags for tossing games.

Books. Use for one of the confederate games. Nine books are placed in three rows of three, one below the other. Confederate is sent from room, group selects book. Leader indicates it by pointing to corner (or middle) of first book he touches, in relation to the position of that book in the setup of threes. (If it is lower left-hand book, he points to that corner of first book.)

Bottle. Spin the Bottle: Group sits in circle, asks bottle a question that can be answered by pointing, like "Who is the best-looking?" "Who is the dumbest?" Bottle is spun; it points its answer. That person then asks a question.

Bottle Caps. (a) For use in tossing games, (b) for holding small amounts of color.

Bottles with Odors. Good opener. Have a number of bottles with distinctive odors, like witch hazel, bay rum, wintergreen, for the game Sense of Smell. See how many people can identify correctly. Put a number on the bottles for easy identification.

Bubble Gum. (a) See who can blow biggest bubble. (For young and old.) (b) Bubble gum art: Chew it up, then model something as with clay. Toothpicks and other implements can be furnished.

Burlap Sacks. Use them for a sack race.

Camouflage Items. The game involves "hiding" objects by placing them on others of same color, same shape, or in a very natural position. Each two players (partners) have a list telling what to look for. When they find an item, they go to one side to record its location. Good for helping folk get acquainted with buildings. Sample items: red comb, penny, gold ring (goes on lamp shades well), dollar bill (in green plants), rubber band (around something), paper clip (on something of same color), black notebook (on something black).

Candles. (a) With teams of equal number in parallel lines, let each run up to a marker and back carrying lighted candle. It must not go out: if so, they must return to starting point to get it lighted. Either use one candle per team or one for each person. (b) Candle Race: Swim with a candle. (c) Candle Bowling: Arrange candles like tenpins, on a table. Stack up enough books that player's chin will be even with candles. Each player gets two blows. Count candles he blows out, as in bowling.

Chalk. Needed in several games, among them—(a) Doodles:

Someone starts a simple figure on the blackboard, shaped like a capital R, for instance. When someone in the group sees how it could be completed into a picture of something or a person, he raises his hand, takes the chalk, and completes picture. Then he starts the next round with an oddly shaped figure (lines, angles, curves permitted). (b) Droodles, as a relay: Two or more teams compete. Players go one at a time to blackboard, draw only one object at a time. The finished product is the figure of a man with head, body, two legs, two arms, two feet. Other objects could be devised. First team through, wins.

Checkers. (a) Play the game, checkers. (b) Use for sliders for a miniature shuffleboard game.

Clock Face on cardboard. For time-telling game. Group picks an hour on the clock face while the leader is not watching. Group takes its own number—4, for instance—and starts counting to itself as leader taps on clock face, until it gets to 20. Group tells him or her to stop—and lo, it is their number! (The leader counts his taps to himself, beginning with one, and taps anywhere on the clock face until the eighth tap. Then he starts at 12 and moves counterclockwise. If group counts correctly, this makes it right every time.)

Coathangers. (a) Good source for strong wire. (b) Profiles: Have the profile of each person traced on a sheet of paper held or thumbtacked to the wall while a strong light is thrown on him to cast the silhouette. Then bend coathanger to coincide with the silhouette.

Combs. Wonderful for a comb band, along with tissue paper.

"Intense Colors" of Chalk, Construction Paper. Excellent for making quick, attractive signs.

Conundrum Cards. Put one conundrum each on many small cards, answer on back. Pass them around to be read aloud and see who can guess the answers. (Excellent collection in *The Fun Encyclopedia.*)

Corks. (a) Good retrieving game in swimming: See who

can get the most corks, all starting at the same time, corks tossed in water. (b) Flip the Cork: Lay one on the top of a coke bottle at edge of table. Each player walks by, arm outstretched straight before him, and without slackening speed, tries to flip the cork off the bottle as he passes by. (c) Ball game: Use large cork and stick for bat, play with softball rules, shorter bases.

Crackers. (a) See who can eat a cracker, and whistle first. (b) Put eggs on floor, show a contestant the eggs, tell him he is to walk around them blindfolded and not crush any. After he is blindfolded, remove eggs, put crackers down instead.

Crafteteria Scraps. Small scraps of craft materials to be made into place cards, favors.

Darts and Board. Paint a targetlike board for darts. Also paint a board for dart baseball. (See *The Fun Encyclopedia.*)

Deck of Cards. For tossing game—try to toss into wastebasket.

Deck Tennis Ring. (a) Use for fun as a tossing game, back and forth. (b) Play Deck Tennis as in instructions coming with game. Get at any sporting goods store. Good for picnics.

Dice. Play Bug or Cootie. Each player rolls, and must get numbers in proper order. I must roll until I get a "1" (for body), then I may use a "2" (for head) or a "4" (for legs). I cannot use "3" (for two antennae) until I have had a "1" and a "2," nor a "5" (tail) until I have the body. Each player gets one roll in rotation. If successful in getting a number he can use, he keeps rolling until he gets a number he cannot use, then passes it on. Each player draws his bug as he accumulates it.

Dried Beans. (a) Use in jar for guessing game. (b) Use as counters by giving each person ten beans, which must be surrendered one at a time if certain conditions are met, such as: (c) Yes or No Taboo: If you are caught during evening saying "yes" or "no," the catcher gets a bean.

Feathers. (a) Keep It Up: Try to blow the feather, keeping it up in the air. Could be played by individuals or by groups, with or without competition. (b) Feather Relay: Equal lines have a feather which they must, one at a time, blow forward to the goal and back. First team that is through, wins. (c) Feather Volleyball: Blow the feather across a net or cord, using volleyball rules.

Finger Painting Equipment. Get the necessary supplies for finger painting at a school supply or art store, and ask there for a demonstration if you don't know how to do it. Easy occupation for large-sized groups.

Funnels, Small Balls. Bounce the balls on the floor, off the wall and catch in funnels. Who can do it the most times out of ten tries?

Golf Tee Tenpins. Knock golf tees down with marbles as a game.

Handkerchiefs. (a) Handkerchief Laugh: Toss one in the air. Everyone must laugh until it hits the floor. Anyone not complying must pay a forfeit, do a stunt. (b) Marker for "Snatch the Handkerchief": Players are in two facing lines, six feet apart, numbered from left to right in their own lines. A handkerchief lies in the exact center between lines. Leader calls, say, for Number Threes, and those two run out to grab the handkerchief and get back to their own lines without being touched. To do so counts a point, and to touch the other player counts a point. (c) Plus and Minus, variation of "Snatch the Handkerchief": When leader calls out, "Four and Five, minus," the Number Ones run out. "Four and Five, plus" would indicate the Number Nines.

Harness Ring, Hook, String. Skill game. Place the hook in the tree, tie harness ring from limb with string so that it will engage the hook. Try to ring the hook the most out of ten tries with the ring. (Get ring and hook at any hardware store.)

Hats. (a) Use in skits, one person acting all parts and putting on a different hat to indicate change of role. (Try in this way the skit "He Ain't Done Right by Nell" in *The Handbook of Skits and Stunts.* (b) Hat Change: Get several players to stand in a circle in front of the rest of the group, each with a hat on his head. Each player reaches out with left hand to hat on neighbor's head. On count "one" by leader each player lifts hat off neighbor's head; on "two," puts it on own head. Leader then shifts and calls for "right hand" and each one simultaneously does same with right hand.

Human Lotto. Draw four lines vertically and four horizontally to divide paper into 25 squares. Each person signs name in squares upon request. After ten minutes play "Lotto." Read out names of those present and keep playing until someone has five in a row. Carry a mimeographed supply of these squares.

Jar Rubbers. Use as tossing game at a board on which are nails or hooks, each one numbered.

Jet Oil or Other Liquid Polish. Makes quickie signs for games, stunts, publicity.

Large-Letter Cards. (a) Use as "flash cards." Divide entire crowd into two groups, then ask for the name of a city beginning with the letter you will display. Then hold up "A." Team having member shouting out first a correct answer gets the card to hold. At end, count up to see who won. Categories could be: cities, villages, counties, rivers, states, countries, famous persons, kings, queens. (Easy way to make: use cardboard from laundered shirts, make letters with liquid shoe polish dauber.) (b) Alphabet Race: Have two teams. Give each player of each team a card. When leader calls out a word, each team tries to spell it correctly first, having players stand in proper order, facing audience. (For list of words see *Handbook for Recreation Leaders* or *The Pleasure Chest.*)

Lifesavers (candy). (a) Use as prizes. (b) Use as relay. Each player has a toothpick in mouth. First person in each line is given lifesaver, which he passes on his toothpick to the next one behind, and so on. Line through first, wins.

List for "Run and Draw" (pencil and paper game). Divide larger group into four smaller ones. Each group sends delegate to leader in center, who assigns something to draw for his group. No words may be spoken. First group yelling out the word gets the point. "Catfish, mailbox, Studebaker car, seventh heaven" are samples.

Magazines. (a) Use pages for making costumes for show or prize. (b) Cut portions that, put together, tell a story. (c) Find ads to act out.

Makeup Kit. Keep one ready for skits and stunts.

Marbles. Marble Roll: Try rolling marbles between bottles without their clinking against bottle. One point for each successful try.

Matches or Toothpicks. (a) Use as counters in games. (b) Fifteen Matches: Two persons play; each may take one, two, or three matches at a time. See who has to take the last match. (c) See who can stack the most matches on top of a milk bottle.

Modeling Clay. Give each person a lump of it and see what he can make.

Nails, Hammer, and Board. This is for a nail-driving contest. See who can drive the nail in to the head in the fewest strokes.

Napkins. (a) Use as folding game gag. Have people fold them several times, then bite on the folded napkin hard. "I knew you'd bite on that one," you say. (b) For making costumes, decorations.

Nature Kit. For Paul Nesbit's game, "Fetchit." Have a number of nature objects (from trees, plants, rocks, pictures of nature things) and place them around the room. Everybody gets a look at them. Divide into two teams, each person having a number on each team. Call for the No. 2's to go and find a picture of a Baltimore oriole. Players involved run to where they think the object is, bring it back to leader. First one back gets point.

Needle and Thread. (a) Use for repairs. (b) Thread the Needle Relay: Each one must run up to a chair ahead of his relay line, thread needle, pull thread out, lay it down on chair or whatever is there, and run back to his place, handing needle to next in line. Team through first, wins. (c) For couples: get wife to sew patch on husband's pants as he lies across her lap.

Nest Eggs, Spoons. For egg relay. In lines, each head person is given a spoon and an egg, which he must carry up to goal and back, then give to next person in line behind him, and so on until whole team is through.

Newspapers. (a) Use for costumes in a contest, using pins, scissors. (b) Use, rolled up, for games. (c) Use opened up, to mark safety spots in tag games.

Paper Bags. (a) Blow up and burst. (b) Use for paper sack puppets. (c) Use as helmets for "football game."

Paper Plates. (a) Decorate them. (b) Play a tossing game. See who can throw "discus" farthest. (c) Use sometimes for containing food!

Pencils and Paper. For all pencil and paper games.

Pieces of Cloth. (a) For costume improvising (using pins). For designing women's hats. (c) For other costume work (sashes, scarves).

Ping-pong Balls, Paddles. (a) Use for indoor softball. Hit with paddle, play as softball. (b) "Football": On a ping-pong table, have two teams, one on each side. Object—to blow ball off other team's side.

Pipe Cleaners. (a) For designing creative figures. (b) For making dolls.

Portable Tether Ball Game.[1] In principle, Tether Ball is a ball on a string, tied to a 10-foot pole. It is a wind-the-pole game.

Postal Cards. (a) Write them to absent members. (b) Pass Through the Card: Cut a slit in the middle, stopping ⅛-inch from each end of the card. Then at ½-inch intervals, cut in almost to the slit in the middle; from the slit, cut out toward outer edges, to form a zigzag pattern. When completed, the card opens up, accordion style, and you can pass through it!

---

[1] See *Games of Skill*, Kit S, 25 cents, Co-operative Recreation Service, Delaware, Ohio.

Pins. Use (a) for costumes, (b) for decorations.

Proverbs on Cards. (a) Read part, let the group fill in the blanks. (b) Give each of several groups a card with a proverb. They assign each member one word of it and have a "signal caller" who stands in front, giving the signal "One, two, three, . . ." and instead of "go" each shouts his word aloud, all blending voices. All except the performing group try to guess what the proverb is. (c) Singing Proverbs: Same as (b), but each must sing his one word to a familiar tune like "Jingle Bells."

Puppets. (a) Hand puppets which you have learned to operate. They can say things to an audience that you wouldn't dare say! (b) Paper sack puppets, made from paper sacks. Get several to help you, put on impromptu play. (Draw faces on paper sacks of different sizes, or paste on cut-out construction paper for eyes, nose, mouth, ears.)

Puzzles. To keep the early comers busy.

Questions and Answers. Have these ready for Truth and Consequences.

Quiz Questions on Cards. (a) Battle of the Sexes: Have questions for men and women, see who wins. Get four each from audience, get men to cheer for men, women for women. (b) It Pays to Be Ignorant: Same idea, but each contestant must give the *wrong answer* to a question. "Is it hot at the North Pole?" "Yes." (c) Other favorite quiz ideas from radio and TV.

Quoits. Use them for tossing game involving pegs.

Read-Aloud Stuff. Copies of books with material to be read aloud for enjoyment of the group, such as: (a) *Ol' Man Adam an' His Chillun,* (b) *Bigger and Better Boners,* (c) *My Tale Is Twisted,* (d) *Cinderella Hassenpfeffer* (Rinehart).

Records, Player. For enjoyment, for rhythmic games.

Rhythm Band Instruments. Use bottles of different sizes, pans, large tin cans—anything that will make a noise. Pick out a rhythmic song and have each "band" member play a different instrument. Both children and adults have fun with this.

Rope Quoits. Take heavy rope, cut in 12- or 15-inch lengths, weave ends together. (a) Chair Leg Toss: Turn chair upside down, toss quoits at the legs. (b) Use for other tossing games involving quoits.

Rubber Heels. (a) Draw a dart target on floor with chalk (or in ground) and toss heels for accuracy and high score. (b) Toss heels into cans, count points for all going into cans, or use horseshoe rules.

Rulers (or mimeographed 6-inch strip). Use for measuring smiles. A prize to the person discovering the person with the biggest smile.

Scissors. (a) Use them as percussion instrument for rhythm band. (b) Crossed or Uncrossed: As players sit in circle, one takes scissors, opens them up, and hands them to next player, saying, "I take the scissors and pass them to you crossed." Each player is to do the same. (The trick—the player crosses or uncrosses his legs.) (c) Use when making decorations or cutting out cloth, or when making newspapers into costumes.

Scotch Tape. For decorations and for repairs.

Scrambles (mimeographed sheets, ready to use). These are letters of words, rearranged and scrambled. Object—to unscramble the most in a given period of time. Scramble (a) names of colleges like "vadrarh" (Harvard), "latune" (Tulane), "esenteens" (Tennessee); (b) girls' names, such as "telivo" (Violet), "tagaremr" (Margaret), "baetilezh" (Elizabeth); (c) famous people, like "soiden" (Edison), "araces" (Caesar), "liurhcclh" (Churchill).

Scrapbooks. Wonderful for early comers to browse through. Have them on such subjects as (a) cartoons, (b) sunsets, (c) babies in various poses, (d) spots of natural beauty.

Sentences for "That's Your Sentence." One at a time, two smooth talkers are assigned outlandish sentences, like "Who put the overalls in Mrs. Murphy's chowder?" and "A penny saved is a penny earned." Swapping sentences, each one talks, and his desire is to say his sentence without being challenged by his opponent with the words, "That's your sentence!" If the opponent challenges correctly, he wins. If the other one completes his stated sentence and goes beyond, he wins.

Sheet. (a) Costume for a ghost. (b) For shadow plays if hung up in doorway with a strong light behind the actors. (c) Backdrop for a short play if held up by two stagehands who stand on chairs. (d) A screen on which to project slides and movies.

Sky Pie. Excellent commercial game with "flying discs." [2] (a) Good tossing game, following instructions. (b) Have two going at same time as contest, tossing. (c) Softball: Arrange teams as in softball. "Batter" takes Sky Pie and tosses it into playing area. (Caught fly is out.) Fielders recover it and play bases as in softball.

Songbooks. Have a supply of some paperbacked song collection—or song sheets—at hand.

Speller. An old-fashioned spelling book for spelling bees.

Spoons. (a) As an "object" to pass. (b) Spoon photography. Send a player from room, select a person. He identifies the person by looking at the picture taken of him on the spoon. (Leader assumes pose of the person chosen, so confederate can tell from that.)

Stick, Curtain Ring, String, Bottle. On a 12-inch stick, tie a 30-inch string, curtain ring on other end of string. Object—holding stick, to make ring go over bottle neck.

Stick for Wrestle Games. (a) Two players grasp broomstick and try to make it turn in the hands of the other. (b) Two players grasp stick, each tries to get it from the other by twisting or pulling. To win, you must have complete possession.

Straws. (a) Use as "pick up sticks." In other words, see how many you can pick up from a pile without moving any others. (b) Give each group a supply, let them build fancy buildings for display later. (c) Shoot toothpicks through them into a pan as a skill game. See how many toothpicks out of ten tries you can get into pan. (d) Bean relay. Each player of a relay

---

[2] Can be secured from Pacific Recreation Service, Inverness, Calif., at $1.

line of six has a straw. He must put a bean on the end of his straw, suck, carry the bean with suction only up to a pan placed several feet ahead, drop bean in the pan, run back and touch the next player in line, who takes his bean up in same fashion. First team through wins.

String, Rope. Use for (a) boundary markers, (b) rope jumping, (c) tug of war, (d) "net" for balloon volley ball, stretching it between two trees for ball to go over it, (e) "ring on a string" game, (f) string relay: each line of six has a ball of string which it must wind around itself, the leader holding the loose end.

Strips of Adding Machine Tape (in 10-inch lengths), *Scissors.* For a race. See who can cut through the tape, beginning to end, first.

Suitcases with Clothes. For suitcase relay. Each suitcase for a line contains identical clothes. One person at a time, must run up to goal, open case, put on clothes, take them off, put in bag, bring bag back to next in line.

Tape Measure. (a) For checking on distance guesses. (b) Measuring Her Waist: Each boy or man guesses how many inches around his partner's waist, then measures to find out.

Tin Cans. (a) Toss corks into them for a skill game. (b) Use as tenpins. (c) Use as receptacles for Washer Tossing game.

Tongue Twisters on Cards. (a) Use just for fun, with several leaders coming forward to try their hand. (b) Use as forfeits in games.

Tunes on Paper. For the game, Hum the Tune. Each person has the title of one tune, which he goes about humming until he finds another with same tune, until a group is formed of those with "Swanee River" or "When You Wore a Tulip," or whatever his tune is. Have these tunes typed or written out, enough sets for everybody.

Washers. Large metal washers from hardware store. Enamel half one color, half another. Sink two tin cans, slightly larger than the washers, into the ground 15 feet apart. Game is played like horseshoes, nearest washers counting one point and those in the can five points. Topped washers in can are canceled, washer for washer. If you have one washer in the can and the two nearest ones outside, your score is 7. Pitch to 21.

Whistle. For those games involving the use of a whistle, refereeing in a ball game (real or mock). (b) For directing swimming, giving instructions to large outdoor group. (c) To signal those who are out of sight in the woods.

4

basic half dozens for fun

Nothing is so important to the the prospective leader of social recreation as to have a basic repertory of games and activities at his instant command. Here is where those classifications or heads for your card file or envelope file are put to use. You may prefer to have other categories, but these six are satisfactory for many leaders: Group Starters, Mixers, Active Games, Less Active Games, Songs and Musical Games, and Stunts.

In training youth leaders for caravan service, the "basic dozen" idea was very effective—that is, each leader selected and familiarized himself with twelve games or activities especially appropriate to each of the six categories and filed the directions on cards. Because space is limited in this book and because we are addressing the book particularly to those who may have only occasional needs for recreational resources, the suggested lists below are limited to a basic half dozen instead of a basic dozen. Leaders can readily amplify their files from the "References" given on pages 63 and 64.

group starters

Purpose: to break the ice at the very beginning of a social affair—often before the majority of the group have arrived. Singing around the piano is excellent at this time.

Animal Barkers. Each person is given a slip of one of four colors. Each color is identified with an animal (dog, for instance), and each animal group has a leader. At a signal all go out to find whatever has been hidden, such as peanuts in the shell. When a player finds one, he must stand over it, giving his animal sound (such as barking) until his captain comes to pick up the peanut.

Big Sneeze. Get one third of the group to say "Hish!", another third to say "Hah!", and the last third to say "Choo!"—then at a signal all say their words together. What a sneeze!

Group Interview. As soon as six or eight persons have come, get each person to introduce himself, tell some facts about himself, and then be ready to answer any questions that any of the group may choose to ask him. As new people arrive, another circle of six chairs can be started.

Mysterious Message. Have some humorous fortunes prepared in advance, written on slips of paper with lemon juice and dried. Pass one to each guest. The heat of a candle brings out the message.

Sense of Smell. Fill a number of bottles with liquids of distinctive odors like witch hazel, wintergreen, Clorox, bay rum, and the like. Number the bottles for easy identification. See how many blindfolded persons can identify the smells correctly.

Who Am I? When the guests first arrive, pin on their backs the name of a famous person. They can ask anyone any questions which can be answered yes or no to give them a clue as to who they are.

mixers

Purpose: To get the crowd circulating around the room, seeing name tags or asking names, getting acquainted.

Even or Odd. Each person is given ten (or more) beans. He goes up to another and asks, "Even or odd?" In his hand are a certain number of beans. If the person guesses correctly he gets the beans. If not, he gives the challenger that many beans. See who gets the most.

Famous Pairs. For pairing off, give each boy the name of the male in a famous couple; a girl, the name of the female. They must look until they find their partners.

I'm Thinking of a Word. Each person as he moves among

the others has the right to say to another, "I'm thinking of a word that rhymes with (chalk)." The other person has three guesses. If he gets the right word, he gets one of the ten beans the other started with; if he fails, he must give up a bean. Each one must have written his chosen word on a slip beforehand.

Measure Smiles. Give each person a mimeographed "ruler" 6 inches long (or a real ruler) and see who can discover the person with the widest smile. Both the discoverer and the discovered get recognition.

Mysterious Stranger. Announce that there is one person in the room who will give to the fifteenth person shaking hands with him a valuable gift. (And of course appoint the mystery man secretly, ahead of time, and supply him with the gift to be awarded.)

Who's Wearing What? Each person is given a mimeographed list of items and is trying to discover who in the room is wearing things like a rope belt, a pair of mismated sox, a charm bracelet, saddle oxfords, Evening in Paris perfume, and so on. List at least ten items, then check up later, and introduce the wearers.

active games

Crows and Cranes. Divide into two equal lines named Crows and Cranes. Beyond each line is a safety line drawn, about 15 feet away from the center line along which they stand beside each other, facing leader. When leader calls "Crows," the crows run toward and beyond their safety line while the cranes try to catch them by touching them. If one is caught, he must join the side which caught him. The object is to reduce the opposite side to no players.

Squirrel in a Cage. Two players face each other, holding hands to form a "tree," with a third person, a "squirrel," standing in the center. There are many trees with squirrels in them, and a few extra squirrels outside. When the leader blows a whistle or yells "Nuts!" the squirrels change trees.

Suitcase Race. Two lines are formed, each with a suitcase containing similar wearing apparel. Each player in each line must run on signal to the goal, open suitcase, put on all clothes, take them off, put them back in suitcase, and bring it back to the next in line—and so on until all in one of the lines are through.

Three-Legged Race. Two persons have the inside ankles tied together with a belt or rope. They must run up to a goal and back, competing with another couple similarly tied.

Tire Change. Each person or each couple stands in a tire, with one or two extra persons or couples outside the tires. When the leader blows the whistle or calls "Change tires!" each player must do so.

Wrestling Match. Two players grasp a broomstick and try to make it turn in the hands of the other. Or, each tries to get the stick completely away from the other by twisting or pulling.

less active games

Black Magic. The group chooses a certain object while one of two confederates is out of the room. The other confederate remains and when the person is called back into the room, points out various articles, asking, "Is it this?" Just before he touches the object chosen by the group he makes sure that he points at some black article.

Bronx Cheer. Someone is sent from the room and the group decides on something he shall do. When he returns, the group directs him by clapping, if he is going in the right direction or doing the right thing, or by booing if he is going in the wrong direction or doing the wrong thing. When he finally succeeds, he may choose someone else to send from the room.

Clap Out Rhythm. The group is divided into two or more sections. Each section claps out the rhythm of a song for the other sections to guess.

Electricity. A circle is formed of not more than thirty persons holding hands. If there are more people present, two circles can be made. One person in the center is It. Someone in the circle starts the "electricity" flowing around by squeezing the hand of the person next to him. That person must pass the squeeze on, quickly. (You can't hold electricity!) "It" keeps watching until he finds the one through whom the electricity is flowing at the moment.

Shouting Proverbs. Give each of several small groups a card on which a proverb is written. They assign to each member one word of the proverb and appoint a signal caller who stands in front, giving the signal, "One, two, three . . ." but instead of the word "go," all members shout their words of the proverb at the same time. The other groups try to guess what the proverb is. A variation is Singing Proverbs, done in the same way, but with each person singing his one word to a familiar tune such as "Jingle Bells," chosen by the group.

Ring on a String. On a 12-inch stick, tie a 30-inch string, with a curtain ring tied on the other end of the string. The object is to hold the stick in such a way as to make the ring go over the neck of a pop bottle.

songs and musical games

Of course, most leaders would have many more than a half dozen or even a dozen songs ready to sing at the right moment, but it is good to have even a few that you are thoroughly familiar with. Here are six that most groups will enjoy. The first five are in *Lift Every Voice;* the sixth is in *357 Songs We Love to Sing.* (See "References," pages 63 and 64.)

"Cindy"	"I'm Gonna Sing"
"Kukuck"	"Marching to Pretoria"
"Ich Bin Ein Musikante"	"Spirit of the Living God"

FOLK GAMES AND SQUARE DANCES

Purpose: To provide musical games that will give people a chance for rhythmic expression, sociability, and exercise; that will create patterns of beauty and demonstrate the fact that other cultural groups have fun, too.

See "References" for source materials to help develop your basic half dozen or dozen. *And Promenade All* is written especially for the beginning leader.

stunts

Purposes: To get as many of the group as possible to take part in one stunt or another and to give the audience an informal good time.

Here are a suggested half-dozen, all found in the Skit and Stunt section of this book. You may want to consult other stunt collections in making up your basic list.

1. *A la Spike Jones.* (Divide group into smaller groups, let each render a song in the manner of Spike Jones.)

2. *The Lie Detector.* An elaborate machine which indicates that the person quizzed is not telling the truth.

3. *Paul Revere's Ride.* He stops in front of a house where an attractive lady invites him in. "To heck with the British!" says Paul.

4. *Style Show.* Especially men in women's clothes.

5. *Too Many Suitors.* (See skit and stunt section.)

6. *Operation Stunt.* A shadow play in which they remove many objects from the victim, including "A can, sir!"

references

books

And Promenade All, Helen and Larry Eisenberg (Fun Books, 5847 Gregory, Hollywood, Calif., $1.00). Singing games, squares, folk games explained for the new leader.

Book of Arts and Crafts, The, Marguerite Ickis and Reba Selden Esh (New York: Association Press, $4.95). All-purpose craft book with a thousand fun-to-make and fun-to-use items from wood, metal, plastics, leather, clay, cloth.

Complete Book of Children's Parties, The (Garden City: Doubleday, $2.00). Excellent source for children's parties, all ages, all situations.

End of Your Stunt Hunt, The, Helen and Larry Eisenberg (Fun Books, 5847 Gregory, Hollywood, Calif., 50 cents).

Family Fun Book, The, Helen and Larry Eisenberg (Association Press, $2.95). Six hundred no-cost or low-cost fun ideas for families.

Folk Party Fun, Gladys Spicer (Association Press, $3.95). Twenty-five completely planned parties for older people, gleaned from rich folk tradition, for homes and groups.

Fun Encyclopedia, The, E. O. Harbin (Nashville, Tenn.: Abingdon-Cokesbury, $3.95). One thousand pages of fun ideas, including a chapter on stunts.

Games from Many Nations, E. O. Harbin (Abingdon-Cokesbury, $1.95). For all ages—149 games from 27 nations.

Grandfather Tales, Richard Chase (Boston: Houghton Mifflin, $2.75). A collection of mountain folk stories.

Handbook of Skits and Stunts, The, Helen and Larry Eisenberg (Association Press, $2.95). Hundreds of skits and stunts for all ages, for auditorium, banquet, camp, party.

Lift Every Voice (Service Dep't, Box 871, Nashville, Tenn., 25 cents). Collection of well-loved songs.

My Tale Is Twisted, Colonel Stoopnagle (New York: Mill-Morrow, $2.50, out of print). Short stories done in "Spoonerism" form (available in libraries).

New Games for 'Tween-Agers, Allan A. Macfarlan (Association Press, $3.00). For pre-teen and teen-agers.

Ol' Man Adam an' His Chillun, Roark Bradford (New York: Harper, $2.75). Tales of the days when "de Lawd" walked the earth like a "nacheral man." The book from which the play "Green Pastures" was written.

Recreation Activities for Adults, National Recreation Association (Association Press, $3.00). Fun activities graded for adult groups.

Recreation for the Aging, Arthur M. Williams (Association Press, $3.00). Successful fun activities for older folk gleaned from nation-wide experience of groups.

Skit Hits, Helen and Larry Eisenberg (Fun Books, 75 cents). A 64-page collection of skits and stunts in paper binding.

Square Dances of Today, Richard Kraus (New York: Barnes, $3.00). One of the better "how-to" texts in this field.

357 Songs We Love to Sing (Chicago: Hall-McCreary, $1.00). Collection of familiar songs with piano accompaniments.

Your Own Book of Campcraft, Catherine Hammett (New York: Pocket Book Junior, 35 cents). Campcraft ideas for youth—written so that they can understand and do them.

play publishers

Walter H. Baker Co., 569 Boylston Street, Boston 16, Mass.

Children's Theatre Press, Anchorage, Ky.

T. S. Denison Publishing Co., 321 Fifth Avenue, S., Minneapolis 5, Minn.

Dramatic Publishing Co., 1706 Prairie Avenue, Chicago 16.

Eldridge Publishing Co., Franklin, Ohio, and Denver, Colo.

Samuel French, Inc., 25 W. 45th Street, New York 36, N. Y.

Northwestern Press, 315 Fifth Avenue, S., Minneapolis 15, Minn.

Row, Peterson & Co., 1911 Ridge Avenue, Evanston, Ill.